TAJIKISTAN 2016 HUMAN RIGHTS REPORT

EXECUTIVE SUMMARY

Tajikistan is an authoritarian state dominated politically by President Emomali Rahmon and his supporters. The constitution provides for a multiparty political system, but the government has historically obstructed political pluralism and continued to do so during the year. A constitutional amendment approved in a national referendum on May 22 outlawed non-secular political parties and removed any limitation on President Rahmon's terms in office as the "Leader of the Nation," allowing him to further solidify his rule.

Civilian authorities only partially maintained effective control over security forces. Officials in the security services and elsewhere in the government acted with impunity.

The most significant human rights problems included citizens' inability to change their government through free and fair elections; torture and abuse of detainees and other persons by security forces; repression, increased harassment, and incarceration of civil society and political activists; and restrictions on freedoms of expression, media, and the free flow of information, including through the repeated blockage of several independent news and social networking websites.

Other human rights problems included torture in the military; arbitrary arrest; denial of the right to a fair trial; harsh and life-threatening prison conditions; prohibition of international monitors' access to prisons; poor religious freedom conditions; violence and discrimination against women; limitations on worker rights; and trafficking in persons, including sex and labor trafficking.

There were very few prosecutions of government officials for human rights abuses.

Section 1. Respect for the Integrity of the Person, Including Freedom from:

a. Arbitrary Deprivation of Life and other Unlawful or Politically Motivated Killings

While the law prohibits extrajudicial killings by government security forces, there were several reports that the government or its agents committed arbitrary or unlawful killings.

On May 19, security officers from the State Committee on National Security in Sughd Region detained a 37-year-old resident of Tursunzoda District, Uktamjon Igamov, on extremism charges. On May 28, he was transferred from the detention center of the State Committee for National Security (GKNB) of Sughd region to Khujand prison. On June 2, Igamov died while in detention in the city prison, allegedly as a result of ill-treatment by law enforcement officials. The cause of death, according to medical examiners, was esophageal and liver failure. Uktamjon Igamov was ill with hepatitis B and was in need of access to medication and medical attention. According to his lawyer, authorities did not provide Igamov proper care, instead mistreating him while he was in custody. His lawyer filed two applications with the regional prosecutor's office to investigate the cause of Igamov's death, but at year's end there was no official response.

b. Disappearance

There were no reports of politically motivated disappearances during the year.

c. Torture and Other Cruel, Inhuman, or Degrading Treatment or Punishment

The constitution prohibits the use of torture. Although the government amended the criminal code in 2012 to add a separate article that defines torture in accordance with international law, there were reports of beatings, torture, and other forms of coercion to extract confessions during interrogations. Officials did not grant sufficient access to information to allow human rights organizations to investigate claims of torture.

On August 4, according to his relatives, Ramazon Zabirov, an 18-year-old recruit with the Border Troops military unit in northern Zafarabad district in Sughd Region, died as a result of beatings by older recruits. Muhammadjon Ulughojaev, a spokesman for the Tajik Border Guards, told Radio Ozodi on August 10 that his office would provide detailed information on the incident after receiving the results of a forensic examination. According to a Radio Ozodi interview given by Zabirov's mother, Mavluda Tagoeva, there were signs of torture on her son's body, including bruises on his chin and head. Tagoeva said that she would ask the Prosecutor General's Office to bring charges against those responsible for her son's death. The Office for Civil Liberties, an NGO that protects the rights of conscripts, provided a lawyer for the Zabirov family.

Prison and Detention Center Conditions

<u>Physical Conditions</u>: The government operated 10 prisons, including one for women, and 12 pretrial detention facilities. Exact conditions in the prisons remained unknown, but detainees and inmates described harsh and life-threatening conditions, including extreme overcrowding and unsanitary conditions. Penal Reform International, an organization conducting prison reform work with regional representation out of Kazakhstan, described the conditions in the women's prison as frigid in the winter with only intermittent electricity and heat, and a lack of food provisions for inmates and staff alike. Disease and hunger were serious problems. UN agencies reported that infection rates of tuberculosis and HIV in prisons were significant and the quality of medical treatment was poor. Authorities often held juvenile boys with adult men.

<u>Administration</u>: A government Office of the Ombudsman exists, and its ombudsman visited prisons but resolved fewer than 2 percent of filed complaints. Nongovernmental organizations (NGOs) reported mistrust of the ombudsman due to the office's loyalty to the president and frequent dismissal of public human rights concerns. A special monitoring group with ombudsmen and NGO representatives conducted announced monitoring visits of prison conditions. No known complaints were filed regarding specific prison conditions.

<u>Independent Monitoring</u>: The Ministry of Justice continued to restrict access to prisons or detention facilities for representatives of the international community. Throughout the year the Coalition against Torture--an association of local NGOs-- and the human rights ombudsman conducted planned visits of closed institutions, although officials denied Coalition against Torture monitors access when they attempted unannounced monitoring visits, private interviews with detainees, or access to internal correctional institution documents. The International Committee of the Red Cross (ICRC) continued to lack access due to the absence of a prison access agreement with the government.

d. Arbitrary Arrest or Detention

The law does not explicitly prohibit arbitrary arrests, which were common. The law states that police must inform the Prosecutor's Office of an arrest within 12 hours and file charges within 10 days. Few citizens were aware of their right to appeal an arrest, and there were few checks on the power of police and military officers to detain individuals.

Role of the Police and Security Apparatus

The Ministry of Internal Affairs, Drug Control Agency (DCA), Agency on State Financial Control and the Fight against Corruption (Anticorruption Agency), State Committee for National Security (GKNB), State Tax Committee, and Customs Service share civilian law enforcement responsibilities. The Ministry of Internal Affairs is primarily responsible for public order and manages the police. The DCA, Anticorruption Agency, and State Tax Committee have mandates to investigate specific crimes and report to the president. The GKNB is responsible for intelligence gathering, controls the Border Service, and investigates cases linked to alleged extremist political or religious activity, trafficking in persons, and politically sensitive cases. The Customs Service reports directly to the president. The Prosecutor General's Office oversees the criminal investigations that these agencies conduct.

Agency responsibilities overlap significantly, and law enforcement organizations defer to the GKNB. Law enforcement agencies were not effective in investigating organized criminal gangs, because the gangs maintained high-level connections with government officials and security agencies. A tacit understanding among law enforcement that certain individuals were untouchable prevented investigations.

Official impunity continued to be a serious problem. While authorities took some limited steps to hold perpetrators accountable, reports of torture and mistreatment of prisoners continued, and the culture of impunity and corruption weakened investigations and prosecutions. In some cases, during pretrial detention hearings or trials judges dismissed defendants' allegations of abuse and torture during detention. Victims of police abuse may submit a formal complaint in writing to the officer's superior or the Office of the Ombudsman. Most victims reportedly chose to remain silent rather than risk official retaliation. The Office of the Ombudsman made few efforts to respond to complaints about human rights violations and rarely intervened, claiming that the office did not have the power to make statements or recommendations regarding criminal cases.

Arrest Procedures and Treatment of Detainees

According to the law, police may detain an individual up to 12 hours before authorities must file criminal charges. If authorities do not file charges after 12 hours, the individual must be released, but police often did not inform detainees of the arrest charges. If police file criminal charges, they may detain an individual 72 hours before they must present their charges to a judge for an indictment hearing. The judge is empowered to order detention, house arrest, or bail pending trial.

According to the law, family members are allowed access to prisoners after indictment, but officials often denied access to attorneys and family members. The law states that a lawyer is entitled to be present at interrogations at the request of the detainee or lawyer, but in many cases, authorities did not permit lawyers timely access to their clients, and initial interrogations occurred without them. Detainees suspected of crimes related to national security or extremism were held for extended periods without being formally charged.

Arbitrary Arrest: The government generally provided a rationale for arrests, but detainees and civil society groups frequently reported that authorities falsified charges or inflated minor incidents to make politically motivated arrests.

On August 22, the General Prosecutor's office detained Jamshed Yorov, the brother of jailed human rights lawyer, Buzurgmehr Yorov. Authorities accused Yorov of leaking the Supreme Court's decision in the secret trial of 13 members of the Islamic Revival Party (IRPT) to an opposition website. Yorov's relatives told RFE/RL on August 29 that the Dushanbe city court ordered that he be detained for two months while he awaited trial for disclosing the documents. Civil society activists reportedly believed the charges were false and were intended to prevent Yorov from leaving the country or defending his brother, who was arrested on fraud, "conspiracy to extremism," and "revolution" charges after he agreed to represent Islamic Revival Party of Tajikistan (IRPT) Deputy Chairman, Mahmadali Hayit. As a part of a general amnesty in September, authorities released Jamshed Yorov.

Some police and judicial officials regularly accepted bribes in exchange for lenient sentencing or release. Law enforcement officials must request an extension from a judge to detain an individual in pretrial detention after two, six, and 12 months.

Pretrial Detention: Defense advocates alleged that prosecutors often held suspects for lengthy periods and registered the initial arrest only when the suspect was ready to confess. In most cases pretrial detention lasted from one to three months, but it could extend as long as 15 months.

Detainee's Ability to Challenge Lawfulness of Detention before a Court: Persons arrested or detained, regardless of charge, are entitled to challenge in court the legal basis or arbitrary nature of their detention. Despite such rights to challenge detention, however, the decrease in the number of lawyers licensed to take on criminal cases and the general apprehension with which lawyers take on sensitive cases limit the use of this entitlement for those arrested on cases suspected to be politically motivated.

Amnesty: On September 10, Zarafo Rahmoni, IRPT member convicted in connection to the September 2015 attacks on a police station and the Dushanbe airport was granted amnesty by presidential decree on the occasion of the 25th anniversary of the country's independence.

e. Denial of Fair Public Trial

Although the law provides for an independent judiciary, the executive branch exerted pressure on prosecutors, defense lawyers, and judges. Corruption and inefficiency were significant problems.

Trial Procedures

Defendants legally are afforded a presumption of innocence, but the presumption did not exist in practice. The courts found nearly all defendants guilty. During the first six months of the year, there were eight acquittals in 6,406 cases. Authorities imposed 10 life sentences during the first half of the year.

Defendants were not always promptly informed of the criminal charges against them or granted a trial without undue delay. Courts generally allowed defendants to be present at their trial and to consult with an attorney in a timely manner during trials but often denied defendants the right to an attorney during the pretrial and investigatory periods, particularly in politically sensitive cases. Authorities leveled politically motivated criminal charges against some defense lawyers to obstruct detained political opposition figures' access to legal counsel and dissuade other lawyers from taking the cases.

On September 29, 2015, authorities arrested Buzurgmehr Yorov, a defense lawyer representing several IRPT members. Authorities accused Yorov of committing large-scale fraud and forgery in business dealings from 2010. Human rights activists and international observers claimed the authorities fabricated the charges to block his defense of the IRPT members and discourage other lawyers from taking the case. On October 15, the General Prosecutor's Office announced it was reclassifying Yorov's case as secret. From May 5 to July 15, Yorov was on trial in the Firdavsi Dushanbe City Court. Although authorities claimed the trial would be open to the public, and allowed international observers to witness the initial hearing, the court subsequently closed the trial to all outside observers except

Yorov's immediate family members. Yorov was also charged with inciting regional and religious enmity, public calls for forcible overthrow of the constitutional order of the country, and public calls for carrying out extremist activity. During the year authorities leveled new charges against him in order to extend his sentence. A final decision was not made in the case before the end of the year.

The government provided attorneys at public expense when requested, but defendants and civil society complained that the government sometimes appointed attorneys as a means to deny defendants' access to the legal counsel of their choice. Defendants and private attorneys said government-appointed attorneys often provided a poor and counterproductive defense. In addition, due to changes in the law on advocates and the establishment of a legal bar, all lawyers were required to retake the bar exam by June 26 in order to renew their licenses. Many lawyers were unable to take the exam in time, in part because there were a limited number of locations offering the exam. Moreover, the government abolished a grandfather clause that would have allowed experienced lawyers to continue to practice. As a result, the number of lawyers accepting criminal defense cases in the country shrunk from approximately 2,000 to only 532. International observers of court cases stated that there were criminal cases in which defendants did not have legal representation.

Defendants may present witnesses and evidence at trial with the consent of the judge. Defendants and attorneys have the right to review all government evidence, confront and question witnesses, and present evidence and testimony, although some defense lawyers claimed the government denied them access to evidential materials collected against their clients. No groups are barred from testifying, and in principle, all testimony receives equal consideration. Courts, however, generally gave prosecutorial testimony far greater consideration than defense testimony. The law extends the rights of defendants in trial procedures to all citizens, and it provides for the right to appeal.

Low wages for judges and prosecutors left them vulnerable to bribery, a common practice. Government officials subjected judges to political influence.

Although most trials are public, the law also provides for secret trials when there is a national security concern. Civil society members faced difficulties in gaining access to high-profile public cases, which the government often declared secret. During the year, the government conducted politically motivated court cases behind closed doors. On February 9, the supreme court began hearing the cases of

13 leading members of the banned Islamic Renaissance Party of Tajikistan (IRPT). The trial was held behind closed doors, as it was classified "secret." The charges against the arrested IRPT members were based on confessions believed by civil society and human rights activists as well as family members of the detained IRPT members to have been obtained under duress. Major international human rights organizations and foreign governments raised concerns over the court hearings, which they alleged failed to ensure due process protections.

Political Prisoners and Detainees

While authorities claimed there were no political prisoners or politically motivated arrests, opposition parties and local and international observers reported the government selectively arrested and prosecuted political opponents. There was no reliable estimate of the number of political prisoners.

On June 2, the Supreme Court sentenced 13 members of the banned Islamic Renaissance Party of Tajikistan (IRPT) to long-term prison sentences for their alleged role in supporting a series of armed attacks led by former Deputy Defense Minister Abduhalim Nazarzoda in Dushanbe and surrounding regions in September 2015, despite lack of credible evidence. The court delivered life sentences to deputy party heads Saidumar Husaini and Mahmadali Hayit. Eleven other high-ranking IRPT activists were sentenced to jail terms ranging from 14 to 28 years. Zarafo Rahmoni, the only woman among those convicted, was sentenced to two years in prison. She was subsequently amnestied and released on September 10, on the occasion of the 25th anniversary of the country's independence. The relatives of the defendants said the defendants pleaded not guilty and asked for lenient sentences. While the government maintained that the convictions are not politically motivated, human rights activists and international human rights groups alleged that the government's intent was to eliminate the IRPT by connecting them to the violent uprising in September 2015.

Civil Judicial Procedures and Remedies

Civil cases are heard in general civil courts, economic courts, and military courts. Judges may order monetary compensation for victims in criminal cases. No separate juvenile justice system exists, although there were some courts that provide a separate room for children linked to the courtroom by video camera.

f. Arbitrary or Unlawful Interference with Privacy, Family, Home, or Correspondence

The constitution states that the home is inviolable. With certain exceptions, it is illegal to enter the home by force or deprive a person of a home. The law states that police may not enter and search a private home without the approval of a judge. Authorities may carry out searches without a prosecutor's authorization in exceptional cases, "where there is an actual risk that the object searched for and subject to seizure may cause a possible delay in discovering it, be lost, damaged, or used for criminal purposes, or a fugitive may escape." The law states that courts must be notified of such searches within 24 hours. Police frequently ignored these laws and infringed on citizens' right to privacy, including personal searches without a warrant.

On November 8, the lower house and upper house of parliament passed amendments to the law on National Security Agencies that increases the power of the State Committee on National Security. Experts state that the President will sign the amendments into law. Under the amendments, security service agents are able to enter homes of private citizens without a warrant or permission in "exceptional cases" involving extremism. According to legal experts, the definition of exceptional cases is taken very broadly, and might allow for a "catch all" that could allow security forces to enter a home for any reason.

According to the law, "when sufficient grounds exist to believe that information, documents, or objects that are relevant to the criminal case may be contained in letters, telegrams, radiograms, packages, parcels, or other mail and telegraph correspondence, they may be intercepted" with a warrant issued by a judge. The law states that only a judge may authorize monitoring of telephone or other communication. Security offices often monitored communications, such as social media and phone calls, without judicial authorization.

Section 2. Respect for Civil Liberties, Including:

a. Freedom of Speech and Press

The law provides for freedom of speech and press, but the government restricted these rights.

<u>Freedom of Speech and Expression</u>: The authorities continued to curb freedom of speech through detentions, prosecutions, the threat of heavy fines, the passage of strict and overreaching slander legislation, and the forced closure of media outlets.

By law a person may be imprisoned for as long as five years for insulting the president.

<u>Press and Media Freedoms</u>: Independent media faced significant and repeated government threats on media outlets. Although some print media published political commentary and investigatory material critical of the government, journalists observed that authorities considered certain topics off limits, including derogatory information about the president or his family, questions about financial improprieties of those close to the president, or content regarding the banned IRPT.

Several independent television and radio stations were available in a small portion of the country, but the government controlled most broadcasting transmission facilities. A decree issued by the government named "guidelines for the preparation of television and radio programs" stipulates that the government through a state broadcast committee has the right to "regulate and control the content of all television and radio networks regardless of their type of ownership."

The government allowed some international media to operate and permitted rebroadcasts of Russian television and radio programs. In November the independent news media outlet *Nigoh* reportedly closed its doors following government harassment and threats of criminal proceedings in response to its prior publication of IRPT content and an inadvertent misspelling of the word "president."

<u>Violence and Harassment</u>: Journalists continued to face harassment and intimidation by government officials. Although the government decriminalized libel in 2012, state officials regularly filed defamation complaints against news outlets in retaliation for publishing stories critical of the government.

On September 19, Ozodagon news agency reported that a journalist from Faraj newspaper, Doro Suhrobi, was beaten by a police officer. While reporting from one of the markets in Dushanbe on the economic difficulties facing the country, Suhrobi was taken to a local police station and detained. According to Suhrobi, he was humiliated and beaten by the police officer that detained him with no intervention from his colleagues. After being released, Suhrobi registered his injuries in a local hospital and filed a complaint with the Ministry of Internal Affairs (MIA). The MIA spokesperson, Umarjoni Emomali, told the media in a press conference that the ministry had launched an investigation into the case.

<u>Censorship or Content Restrictions</u>: Journalists regularly practiced self-censorship to avoid retribution from officials. Opposition politicians had limited or no access to state-run television. The government gave opposition parties minimal broadcast time to express their political views, while the president's party had numerous opportunities to broadcast its messages. Access to information was particularly difficult for journalists in the weeks prior to the May 22 Constitutional Referendum. State run TV and radio stations did not broadcast any programs on their channels offering views in opposition to the constitutional amendments.

Newspaper publishers reported the government exercised restrictions on the distribution of materials, requiring all newspapers and magazines with circulations exceeding 99 recipients to register with the Ministry of Culture. The government continued to control all major printing presses and the supply of newsprint. Independent community radio stations continued to experience registration and licensing delays that prevented them from broadcasting. The government restricted issuance of licenses to new stations, in part through an excessively complex application process. The National Committee on Television and Radio, a government organization that directly manages television and radio stations in the country, must approve and then provide licenses to new stations. The government continued to deny the BBC a renewal of its license to broadcast on FM radio.

<u>Libel/Slander Laws</u>: In 2012 the government repealed the law criminalizing libel and defamation and downgraded the offenses to civil violations, although the law retains controversial provisions that make publicly insulting the president an offense punishable by a fine or up to five years in jail. Nevertheless, libel judgments were common, particularly against newspapers critical of the government.

Internet Freedom

Individuals and groups faced extensive government surveillance of internet activity, including e-mails, and often self-censored their views while posting on the internet. According to 2016 Telecommunications data, 19.5 percent of the population of Tajikistan used the internet in that year.

There were new and continuing government restrictions on access to internet websites, such as Facebook, YouTube, Google, Google services, and Radio Free Europe/ Radio Liberty. The State Communications Service (SCS) routinely denied involvement in blocking these sites, but the government admitted to periodically implementing a law that allows interruption of internet content and telecommunications "in the interest of national security." The government continued to implement a 2015 law enabling the State Committee for National Security (GKNB) to shut off internet and telecommunications during security operations.

Since May, independent news agency websites *Asia-Plus*, *Radio Liberty's Tajik Service* and *Ozodagon* were inaccessible in the country. Local experts said the government blocked these websites to limit and control coverage of the constitutional referendum. Previously, access to most social media networks, such as Facebook, YouTube, Odnoklasniki, and numerous news agency websites, were blocked intermittently throughout the year.

Academic Freedom and Cultural Events

The Ministry of Education maintained a dress code that bans wearing the hijab in schools and government institutions. Authorities allowed women to wear a traditional version of the head covering--a scarf that covers hair but not the neck--to schools and universities. Many female students wore the hijab to and from school but removed it upon entering the school building. Parents and school officials appeared to accept this arrangement. The ministry also maintained its ban on beards for all teachers. Students with beards reported being removed from class, questioned, and asked to shave.

A Ministry of Education directive requires school administrators to inform students of the Law on Parental Responsibility, which bans all persons under age 18 from participating in public religious activities, with the exception of funerals. The law provides that, with written parental consent, minors between the ages of seven and 18 may obtain a religious education during their free time from school and outside the state education curriculum and may worship as part of educational activities at religious institutions.

The government requires all persons studying religion abroad to register with the Committee on Religious Affairs (CRA), Ministry of Education, and Ministry of Foreign Affairs. The law provides criminal penalties for violating restrictions on sending citizens abroad for religious education, preaching and teaching religious doctrines, and establishing ties with religious groups abroad without CRA consent.

The Ministry of Education banned students from attending events sponsored by or conducted for foreign organizations during school hours.

There were several reports throughout the year that academics writing on sensitive subjects regarding politics, religion, and history feared publishing or even submitting their articles for review for fear of retribution. There was no official censorship, however, of films, plays, art exhibits, music presentations, or other cultural activities.

b. Freedom of Peaceful Assembly and Association

Freedom of Assembly

The constitution provides the right to freedom of assembly, but the government required that individuals obtain permission from the government to stage public demonstrations. Individuals considering staging peaceful protests reportedly chose not to do so for fear of government reprisal. On September 19, the families of exiled opposition figures protesting in Warsaw reported retaliatory law enforcement harassment and detention at their homes in Tajikistan.

On May 15, approximately 200-300 individuals organized a celebration in honor of the Indian holiday "Holi" in the local stadium "Spartak," a central Dushanbe building belonging to the MIA. Organizers of the event told human rights activists they obtained an official permit from the MIA to hold the event in the stadium and that it was the fourth time the group celebrated this holiday in Dushanbe. As the celebration neared its conclusion, the crowd of mostly minors were exiting the stadium when police arrived and forcefully detained approximately 200 participants. The detainees reported they were verbally abused for celebrating a non-Muslim holiday, beaten, and threatened with rape. Some of the detainees recorded the incident and later posted the recordings on social media. NGO Civil Liberties filed a complaint with the MIA on behalf of the detainees, but the alleged victims never subsequently submitted a formal request for an investigation.

Freedom of Association

The constitution protects freedom of association, but the government restricted this right. Civil society organizations reported a noticeable increase in the number and intensity of registration and tax inspections by authorities. The government continued to enforce the ban on activities held under the banner of the IRPT. As a result of the May 22 constitutional referendum, non-secular political parties became illegal.

On March 30, the government adopted new regulations to the Law on Public Associations that indicated how organizations registered with the Ministry of Justice (MOJ) must inform the MOJ of their foreign funding. Shortly after the MOJ adopted the regulations, the ministry discussed them publicly with members of civil society and donor organizations. The MOJ created a working group, which included NGO representatives, to consider possible changes to the form NGOs must submit to notify the government of their foreign funding. On June 9, the MOJ approved a new form, based in part upon the suggestions of NGO representatives. The president signed the new regulations into law on August 8. International human rights organizations and NGOs criticized the regulations, saying they created an unnecessary burden on NGOs and that the MOJ did not have the capacity to process all the information it would receive from organizations.

c. Freedom of Religion

See the Department of State's *International Religious Freedom Report* at www.state.gov/religiousfreedomreport/.

d. Freedom of Movement, Internally Displaced Persons, Protection of Refugees, and Stateless Persons

In-country Movement: The law provides for freedom of movement, but the government imposed some restrictions. The government prohibits foreigners, except diplomats and international aid workers, from traveling within a 15-mile zone along the borders with Afghanistan and China in the Khatlon Region and the Gorno-Badakhsan Autonomous Oblast (GBAO) unless they obtain permission from the Ministry of Foreign Affairs. Officials did not always enforce the restrictions along the western border with Afghanistan, although the government continued to require travelers (including international workers and diplomats) to obtain special permits to visit the GBAO. The government also continued to enforce a policy barring Afghan refugees from residing in urban areas.

Protection of Refugees

Access to Asylum: The law provides for the granting of asylum or refugee status, and the government has established a system for providing protection to refugees. Nevertheless, the process for making asylum status determinations remained uncertain, lacking transparency, and administrative and judicial procedures did not comply with international standards. Although not required by law, government officials required refugees and asylum seekers to obtain a visa and a valid travel document before entering the country. Government officials without due process detained and deported individuals not in possession of a visa.

The government processed asylum applications through the National Refugee Status Determination Commission and granted applicants documents to regularize their stay and prevent deportation. Formal notifications of administrative and legal decisions provide little insight into the rationale for adjudications. In some instances, when denying claimants refugee status, officials cited, in broad terms, a lack of evidence of persecution in the refugee's home country or "malpractice" on the part of refugees applying to renew their status, such as violation of the prohibition of living in big cities, including in Dushanbe. Unofficially, some refugees claimed authorities could deny cases if sufficiently high bribes were not paid.

The government continued to place significant restrictions on claimants, and officials continued to enforce a law decreed in 2000 prohibiting asylum seekers and refugees from residing in the capital and all major cities in the country. Security officials regularly monitored refugee populations. Asylum seekers and refugees regularly reported to UNHCR that security officials harassed them, often for allegedly lacking personal identification, and attempted to extort money. Police subjected them to raids if police believed they were residing in prohibited areas.

During the first seven months of the year the government deported five asylum seekers and refugees to Afghanistan. The deportees included rejected asylum seekers and refugees with revoked status based on violation of the law prohibiting such persons from residing in urban areas as well as cumbersome preconditions that preclude a claimant from registering as a refugee. Most of the cases of revoked status were under appeal in court with the support of UNHCR. The deportations took place despite the incomplete appeal processes. In some of these cases, there was risk of refoulement.

Although the law stipulates that refugee status be granted for as long as three years, the transfer of refugee processing to the Ministry of Internal Affairs in 2009 resulted in much shorter periods of status being granted. According to government statistics, the country had 2,185 registered refugees, 98 percent of whom were Afghan. An additional 141 asylum seekers, mostly Afghan, were seeking refugee status.

Freedom of movement: Refugees are not permitted to live in major urban areas, including Dushanbe, according to Government Resolution 325, restricting their ability to find work and go to school.

Employment: An increasing percentage of refugees entering the country did not possess professional backgrounds or job skills, and many faced discrimination by the local population. The requirement to live outside urban areas created additional problems for finding adequate work. While UNHCR assisted some female refugees by providing vocational job training in skills such as sewing, cooking, and hairdressing, most female refugees remained in the home in accordance with traditional cultures. Most male refugees worked for small enterprises.

Access to Basic Services: Refugees and asylum seekers are legally entitled to education and health services alongside local citizens. The Ministry of Education allowed Afghan parents to send their children to local schools without paying fees. UNHCR partners provided books, school uniforms, and some language classes to these children and assisted with their medical expenses. The law provides registered refugees with equal access to law enforcement, health care, and the judicial system, although refugees did not always have equal access. In practice, refugees were subject to harassment, discrimination, and extortion.

Durable Solutions: Following the amended Law on Nationality adopted in August, refugees hold equal standing to non-refugee foreigners when applying for citizenship. Although the government and UNHCR agreed on local integration of refugees into the general population as a more durable solution to the refugee situation, there was little progress in processing pending cases to completion.

Stateless Persons

As of July a reported 769 persons registered as stateless by the government. As of October 2016 UNHCR and its partners identified and registered as many as 23,150 individuals at risk of statelessness in three pilot provinces, (Khatlon, Sughd, and District of Republic Subordination), highlighting the potential extent of statelessness as well as the challenges and opportunities of facilitating solutions. Holders of former Soviet Union passports constituted the bulk of those at risk of statelessness, although a number of people, predominantly women, holding expired foreign passports came forward and sought counselling.

Section 3. Freedom to Participate in the Political Process

The law provides citizens the ability to choose their government in free and fair periodic elections based on universal and equal suffrage, but the government restricted this right. The president and his supporters continued to dominate the government while taking steps to ensure the elimination of genuine pluralism in the interest of consolidating power. The president's political party, the People's Democratic Party of Tajikistan (PDPT), dominated both houses of parliament. PDPT members held most government positions. The president had broad authority, which he exercised throughout the year, to appoint and dismiss officials.

Elections and Political Participation

Recent Elections: On May 22, the government held a national referendum on 41 proposed amendments to the constitution. Citizens were required to vote "yes" or "no" on the full package and were unable to cast votes on each of the 41 proposed amendments. According to the Central Commission for Elections and Referenda (CCER) 4,039,183 citizens voted, constituting 92 percent of the total list of registered voters. Results from the CCER indicated that 3,814, 477 people (94.5 percent) voted in favor of the amendments, and 134,171 (3.3 percent) voted against. Anecdotal evidence, commentary on social media, and media reports indicated that voter turnout was actually quite low, an indication that the government inflated the vote count.

According to the CCER, 7,500 local observers from political parties, youth unions, trade unions, and public organizations monitored the referendum, as did 120 international observers from the Commonwealth of Independent States (CIS), Shanghai Cooperation Organization, and CIS inter-parliamentary assembly. Organization for Security Cooperation in Europe's Office for Democratic Institutions and Human Rights did not deploy an observation mission for the referendum.

Several prominent news outlets, including Ozodagon, Faraj, and Tojnews did not report on the referendum at all. Despite this, one week prior to the referendum, the State Communications Service ordered internet service providers in the country to block access to the websites of independent news agencies Asia Plus, Ozodagon, and Ozodi.

Out of 40 amendments, there were three significant changes to the constitution. One amendment institutionalized into the constitution the title of "Leader of the Nation" upon President Rahmon--a title given to Rahmon by law in December

2015 but requiring confirmation through amendment of the constitution. This title removed term limits for President Rahmon and gave him lifelong immunity from judicial and criminal prosecution. A second amendment lowered the eligible age to run for president from 35 to 30 years, leading to speculation that the amendment is intended to open a path for the president's son, Rustam Emomali, to run for president in the next presidential elections, scheduled for 2020, when he will be 33. A third amendment banned all non-secular political parties.

Political Parties and Political Participation: Seven major political parties, including the PDPT, were legally registered. Opposition political parties had moderate popular support and faced high levels of scrutiny from the government. All senior members of President Rahmon's government were PDPT members. Most members of the country's 97-seat parliament were members of the PDPT, pro-government parties, or PDPT-affiliates.

Participation of Women and Minorities: Women were under-represented in decision-making processes at all levels of political institutions. Female representation in all branches of government was less than 30 percent. There was one female minister but no ministers from minority groups. The deputy prime minister, a female, was removed from her position after reaching retirement age early in the year. Cultural practices discouraged participation by women in politics, although the government and political parties made efforts to promote their involvement, such as the 1999 presidential decree that mandated every ministry or government institution have a female deputy. Civil society criticized this decree as a barrier to women holding top government positions.

Section 4. Corruption and Lack of Transparency in Government

The law provides criminal penalties for corruption by officials, but the government did not implement the law effectively. Officials frequently engaged in corrupt practices with impunity. Corruption, nepotism, and regional hiring bias were pervasive at all levels of government.

Corruption: Corruption in the Education Ministry was systemic. Prospective students were required to pay thousands of somoni (hundreds of dollars) in bribes to enter the country's most prestigious universities, and provincial colleges required several hundred somoni. Students often paid additional bribes to receive good examination grades.

Many traffic police retained fines they collected for violations. Traffic police posted at regular intervals along roads arbitrarily stopped drivers to ask for bribes. The problem was systemic in part due to the low official wages paid to traffic police. Many traffic police reportedly paid for their jobs, an expense they tried to recoup by extracting bribes from motorists.

The Ministry of Internal Affairs, Anticorruption Agency, and Prosecutor General's Office are responsible for investigating, arresting, and prosecuting suspected corrupt officials. The government acknowledged a problem with corruption and took some steps to combat it, including putting lower-level officials on trial for taking bribes.

Both the Ministry of Internal Affairs and the Anticorruption Agency submit cases to the Prosecutor General's Office at the conclusion of their investigations. In some instances, the agency collaborated with the Prosecutor General's Office throughout the entire process.

The prosecutor general investigated some cases of suspected corruption by government employees, but the bulk of the cases involved mid- or lower-level officials, and none involved large-scale abuses. There were instances of the Prosecutor General's Office suddenly dropping cases submitted by the Ministry of Internal Affairs or the Anticorruption Agency.

In July authorities suspended a fraud investigation against Najmiddinov Saidov, the brother of the Head of the Customs Service of Tajikistan, Lieutenant General Abdufattoh Goibov. In October 2015 media reported that the State Committee on National Security arrested Saidov while he was taking a bribe in the amount of 2.6 to 4 million somoni ($330,000 to $506,000). According to widespread media reports, Saidov took the bribe in exchange for a promised position as the Head of the Customs Office in one of the districts. Saidov, who served as the head of the branch office of "Tojiksodirotbank" in Dangara district, was fined 200,000 somoni ($25,500 dollars) and was released from detention.

Financial Disclosure: Public officials are not subject to financial disclosure laws.

Public Access to Information: Public budgets, particularly those involving major state-owned enterprises, lacked transparency. Although parliament has oversight of the state budget, it passed annual budgets almost without comment despite large, unexplained, and undefined expenses. Each year the government releases a report on budget performance for the previous year that contains numerous details about

education, health, and other social sector spending. A considerable amount of
government spending, including that for major buildings, parks, and other special
projects such as summer residences for the president, occurred off budget.

**Section 5. Governmental Attitude Regarding International and
Nongovernmental Investigation of Alleged Violations of Human Rights**

Domestic human rights groups encountered increased difficulty monitoring and
reporting on the general human rights situation in the country. Domestic NGOs
and journalists were careful to avoid public criticism of the president or other high-
ranking officials and refrained from discussing issues connected to the banned
IRPT. Human rights and civil society NGOs faced increasing pressure from the
government. Authorities investigated a number of NGOs for alleged registration
problems and administrative irregularities.

The United Nations or Other International Bodies: The government generally
cooperated with international NGOs. It facilitated visits by high-ranking officials
from the UN, the OSCE, Human Rights Watch, and other international
organizations but continued to deny the International committee of the Red Cross
access to prison facilities.

Government Human Rights Bodies: The Office of the Human Rights Ombudsman
made little effort to respond to complaints from the public during the year, and its
limited staff and budget further constrained its capacity to do so. The
ombudsman's office met with NGOs to discuss specific human rights cases and
general human rights problems in the country, but no government action resulted.
In May the Ministry of Justice gave NGOs the opportunity to discuss further
implementing regulations to amendments to the Law on Public Associations and
incorporated some of their recommendations into the final draft, but human rights
NGOs report continuing politically motivated government interference in their
activities under the auspices of the law.

The government's Office for Constitutional Guarantees of Citizens' Rights
continued to investigate and answer citizens' complaints, but staffing inadequacies
and inconsistent cooperation from other governmental institutions hampered the
office's effectiveness. The procedural code on administrative offenses provided
procedural protections to those persons accused of minor offenses.

Section 6. Discrimination, Societal Abuses, and Trafficking in Persons

Women

<u>Rape and Domestic Violence</u>: The law prohibits rape, which is punishable by up to 20 years' imprisonment. There was no separate statute for spousal rape. The government did not provide statistics on the number of cases or convictions. Law enforcement officials usually advised women not to file charges but registered cases at the victim's insistence. Most observers believed the majority of cases were unreported because victims wished to avoid humiliation.

Domestic violence does not have its own statute in the criminal code. Violence against women, including spousal abuse, remained a widespread problem. According to a survey conducted by the National Statistic Committee in 2015, 19 percent of women between ages 15 and 49 reported they experienced physical violence since age 15. Women underreported violence against them due to fear of reprisal or inadequate response by police and the judiciary, resulting in virtual impunity for the perpetrators. Authorities wishing to promote traditional gender roles widely dismissed domestic violence as a "family matter." Women and girls were more vulnerable to domestic violence because of early and unregistered marriages.

Five police stations were fully equipped and staffed with police officers trained, with OSCE support, to respond to family violence cases and address the needs of victims in a gender-sensitive manner. In rural areas the government and NGOs operated additional crisis centers and hotlines where women could seek guidance on domestic violence problems and legal assistance, but many of these centers lacked funding and resources. Local governments donated the premises of three of the shelters. The Committee for Women's Affairs (within the government) had limited resources to assist domestic violence victims, but local committee representatives referred women to the crisis shelters for assistance.

In 2012 the government adopted a law on domestic violence that is in line with internationally accepted standards; however, the implementing mechanism was inadequate. The Ministry of Internal Affairs lacked the capacity and training to implement the law, although it worked with the international community to increase capacity. In May 2014, the government adopted an action plan to implement domestic violence law. The plan calls for law enforcement, court officials, the prosecutor's office, and representatives of relevant government bodies to receive training on their responsibility to combat domestic violence. The plan also calls for greater cooperation between law enforcement officials and local leaders to change societal attitudes towards domestic violence. The government took some steps to collect information on domestic violence, but many cases of domestic abuse went unreported. In April the government adopted official implementing instructions for the Ministry of Internal Affairs on how to refer and register cases of domestic violence, while not having a particular criminal statute to draw from to do so. Domestic violence incidents were registered under general violence and hooliganism, with a special notation in paperwork indicating a distinction for domestic violence.

Authorities seldom investigated reported cases of domestic violence, and they prosecuted few alleged perpetrators. The Ministry of Internal Affairs is authorized to issue administrative restraining orders, but by law police cannot act without a written complaint from the victim, even if there were other witnesses. Consequently, police often gave only warnings, short-term detentions, or fines for committing "administrative offenses" in cases of domestic violence.

Physical and psychological abuse of wives by mothers-in-law was widespread. In some rural areas, officials observed a continued trend of female suicide in which independent observers considered such abuse to be a contributing cause.

Sexual Harassment: No specific statute banned sexual harassment in the workplace. Victims often did not report incidents because of fear of social stigma. Authorities often perceived sexual harassment as female fabrications. Women reporting sexual harassment faced retaliation from their employers as well as scrutiny from their families and communities.

Reproductive Rights: The government did not interfere with the rights of individuals and couples to decide freely and responsibly the number, spacing, and timing of their children; to manage their reproductive health; and to have the information and means to do so, free from discrimination, coercion, and violence. Traditional stereotypes prevented women and girls from obtaining information on reproductive health and access to services. According to UN data, 87 percent of births were attended by skilled health personnel and 31 percent of women of reproductive age used a modern method of contraception in 2016. An estimated 22 percent of women reported an unmet need for family planning.

Discrimination: Although the law provides for men and women to receive equal pay for equal work, cultural barriers restricted women's professional opportunities (see section 7.d.). According to the World Bank report, *Women, Business, and the Law 2014*, women and men have equal ownership rights to property, although women owned significantly less property than men. The extensive number of male migrant workers to Russia and other parts of Central Asia, many of whom failed to send remittances or return home, exacerbated economic pressures on women, who had to provide for themselves and their children, and resulted in a significant gender imbalance in the population.

Due to family pressure, young women, especially adolescent girls, often dropped out of school to marry. The law protects women's rights in marriage and family matters, but families often pressured female minors to marry against their will. Religious marriages were common substitutes for civil marriages, due to the high marriage registration fees associated with civil marriages and the power afforded men under religious law. In cases of religious marriages not registered with the government, husbands simply repeated a phrase in front of two witnesses to divorce their wives. Husbands also used these officially unregistered religious marriages to prevent wives from accessing family assets and other rights in the event of divorce. The practice of men divorcing their wives by sending text messages declined after the 2011 Council of Ulema fatwa (religious edict) declared the practice unacceptable.

The 2004 Council of Ulema fatwa prohibiting Hanafi Sunni women--constituting the vast majority of the female population--from praying in mosques remained in effect. Religious ceremonies also made polygyny possible, despite the illegality of the practice. NGOs estimated that up to 10 percent of men practiced polygyny. Many of these polygynous marriages involved underage brides. Unofficial second and third marriages were increasingly common, with neither the wives nor their children having legal standing or rights.

Inheritance laws do not discriminate against women, although some inheritances passed disproportionately to sons. In addition, many men hid their assets with their parents or other family members, so that if divorce occurred, they could claim no wealth and become exempt from paying child support or other restitution to the former wife.

The Ministry of Internal Affairs supported programs to increase the representation of female officers in law enforcement.

Children

Birth Registration: Children derive citizenship by birth within the country's territory and from their parents. The government is required to register all births.

Many parents waited to register a birth until a child was ready to enter school, since birth registration is required to receive public services such as education.

Education: Free and universal public education is compulsory until age 16 or completion of the ninth grade. The UN Children's Fund (UNICEF) reported that school attendance generally was good through the primary grades, but girls faced disadvantages, especially in rural school systems where families elected to keep them home after primary grades to take care of siblings or work in agriculture. Families often invested money in their sons' education rather than that of their daughters so that the boys, with a better education, could provide for them and take care of their parents in old age.

According to a 2015 study conducted by the UN Women subdivision of the UN, dropout rates were higher among women. The analysis found that at the end of compulsory education, girls averaged 26.2 percent dropout rates, while their male counterparts averaged 21.6 percent.

Child Abuse: The Committee on Women and Family Affairs and regional child rights protection departments are responsible for addressing problems of violence against children. Girls subjected to violence could receive support from several centers throughout the country. The Women of Science of Tajikistan Association, supported by UNICEF and the Dushanbe mayor's office, organized a hotline for free legal and psychological consultations for girls who were victims of violence. There were some cases in which boys who were victims of violence were also able to use the hotline to access legal and psychosocial services. Funding for and the capacity of such programs were limited. A five-year program for a Girls Support Center ended in its second year due to lack of funding.

Early and Forced Marriage: The legal minimum age for marriage of men and women is 18 years. Under exceptional circumstances, which a judge must determine, such as in the case of pregnancy, a couple may also apply to a court to lower the marriageable age to 17. Underage religious marriage was more widespread in rural areas. Many parents told their daughters to quit school after ninth grade, at which point parents considered their daughters to have obtained sufficient professional skills, such as sewing or cooking, to have a source of income in the future.

The law expressly prohibits forced marriages of girls under age 18 or entering into a marriage contract with a girl under 18. Early marriage carries a prison sentence of up to six months, while forced marriage is punishable by up to five years' imprisonment. In most cases the law punishes underage marriage with a fine. Because couples may not register a marriage where one of the would-be spouses is under age 18, many simply have a local religious leader perform the wedding ceremony. Without a civil registration certificate, the bride has few legal rights.

NGOs claimed that during the year regional ministries of education and schoolteachers were very actively involved in persuading parents not to take their daughters out of school. The NGOs claimed the situation in some rural areas had improved, and the government partially addressed the problem by requiring mullahs to demand a certificate of civil marriage registration to conduct the religious ceremony; however, this regulation was not effectively enforced, and mullahs conducted religious marriages at unmonitored private ceremonies.

Sexual Exploitation of Children: The law prohibits the commercial sexual exploitation of children and child pornography. Law enforcement bodies investigated cases of commercial sexual exploitation of children, but no statistics were available on the number of prosecutions or convictions. The minimum age of consensual sex is 16 years. According to an NGO working with victims of domestic violence, sexual exploitation, and sex trafficking, there were several cases in which family members or third parties forced children into sex work in nightclubs and in private homes.

International Child Abductions: The country is not a party to the 1980 Hague Convention on the Civil Aspects of International Child Abduction. See the Department of State's *Annual Report on International Parental Child Abduction* at www.travel.state.gov/content/childabduction/en/legal/compliance.html.

Anti-Semitism

There were no reports of anti-Semitic acts. The small Jewish community had a place of worship and faced no overt pressure from the government or other societal pressures. Emigration to other counties continued.

Trafficking in Persons

See the Department of State's *Trafficking in Persons Report* at www.state.gov/j/tip/rls/tiprpt/.

Persons with Disabilities

The law on social protection of persons with disabilities applies to individuals having physical or mental disabilities, including sensory and developmental disabilities. The law prohibits discrimination against persons with disabilities in employment, education, access to health care, and provision of other state services, but public and private institutions generally did not commit resources to implement the law. The law requires government buildings, schools, hospitals, and transportation, including air travel, to be accessible to persons with disabilities, but the government did not enforce these provisions.

Many children with disabilities were not able to attend school because doctors did not deem them "medically fit." Children deemed medically unfit could attend special state-run schools specifically for persons with physical and mental disabilities. Observers noted that the capacity of these institutions probably did not meet demand. Mainstream schools and state-run schools for persons with physical and mental disabilities used the same curriculum. Doctors decided which subjects students were capable of studying, and directors of state-run schools could change the requirements for students to pass to the next grade at their discretion. Some children with Down syndrome and autism were allowed to attend mainstream schools. Up to 10 percent of families kept children with disabilities at home and provided home education or tutors.

The government charges the Commission on Fulfillment of International Human Rights, the Society of Invalids, and local and regional governmental structures with protecting the rights of persons with disabilities. Although the government maintained group living and medical facilities for persons with disabilities, funding was limited, and facilities were in poor condition.

National/Racial/Ethnic Minorities

There were occasional reports that some law enforcement officials harassed ethnic Afghans and Uzbeks.

Acts of Violence, Discrimination, and Other Abuses Based on Sexual Orientation and Gender Identity

While same-sex sexual conduct is legal in the country, and the age of consent is the same as for heterosexual relationships, the law does not provide legal protection against discrimination. Homophobic attitudes and little societal tolerance toward lesbian, gay, bisexual, transgender, and intersex (LGBTI) persons made it rare for individuals to disclose their sexual orientation or gender identity. Throughout the country there were reports that LGBTI individuals faced physical and psychological abuse, harassment, extortion, and exploitation on pain of revealing their LGBTI status to their families, including perpetrated by police.

There is no law against discrimination based on sexual orientation or gender identity, and LGBTI persons were victims of police harassment and faced threats of public beatings by community members. Public activism on behalf of LGBTI persons was limited. LGBTI representatives claimed law enforcement officials extorted money from LGBTI persons by threatening to tell their employers or families of their activities and in some cases subjected LGBTI persons to sex trafficking. Hate crimes against members of the LGBTI community reportedly went unaddressed. LGBTI representatives claimed health-care providers discriminated against and harassed LGBTI persons. LGBTI advocacy and health groups reported harassment from government officials and clergy, to include violent threats, as well as obstruction of their activities by the Ministry of Health.

In May 2015 the Global Fund to Fight AIDS, Tuberculosis, and Malaria released a report stating that there were 30,000 LGBTI individuals in the country. The Ministry of Health refuted the data, saying that in reality the number was much lower, but provided no statistic.

It was difficult for transgender persons to obtain new official documents from the government. The law allows for changing gender in identity papers if a medical organization provides an authorized document. Because a document of this form does not exist, it was difficult for transgender persons to change their legal identity to match their gender. This created internal problems involving any activity requiring government identification, including the acquisition of a passport for international travel.

HIV and AIDS Social Stigma

There was societal discrimination against individuals with HIV/AIDS. According to a 2014 demographic and health survey, 73 percent of individuals reported discriminatory attitudes towards those with HIV. In March 2014 President Rahmon signed amendments to the law on entry, stay, and residence for persons with HIV. The amendments remove mandatory HIV testing for foreigners, thereby eliminating all HIV-related restrictions on entry, stay, and residence.

The government offered HIV testing free of charge at 140 facilities, and partner notification was mandatory and anonymous. The World Health Organization noted officials systematically offered HIV testing to prisoners, military recruits, street children, refugees, and persons seeking visas, residence, or citizenship.

Women were increasingly vulnerable to HIV infection because of social taboos on discussion of sex education topics and popular sentiment against the use of condoms. Women remained a minority of those infected with HIV, although their incidence of infection was increasing. The government's National Center on HIV, under the Ministry of Health, detected 515 cases of HIV infection during the first half of the year, of which 325 were male and 190 were female. There were 8,224 officially registered cases of HIV in the country, 5,996 of which involved men and 2,628 involved women.

Section 7. Worker Rights

a. Freedom of Association and the Right to Collective Bargaining

The law provides for the right to form and join independent unions but requires registration for all NGOs, including trade unions. The law also provides that union activities, such as collective bargaining, be free from interference except "in cases specified by law," but the law does not define such cases. Workers have the right to strike, but the law requires that meetings and other mass actions have prior official authorization, limiting trade unions' ability to organize meetings or demonstrations. The law provides for the right to organize and bargain collectively, but it does not specifically prohibit antiunion discrimination.

Workers joined unions, but the government used informal means to exercise considerable influence over organized labor, including influencing the selection of labor union leaders. The government-controlled umbrella Federation of Trade Unions of Tajikistan did not effectively represent worker interests. There were reports that the government compelled some citizens to join state-endorsed trade unions and impeded formation of independent unions. According to International Labor Organization figures, 1.3 million persons belonged to unions. There were no reports of antiunion discrimination during the year.

Citizens were reluctant to strike due to fear of government retaliation.

In December 2015 three dozen female workers employed by the government-owned utility company, "Niholparvari va Kabudizorkuni" gathered at the local government administration of Kulob city and demanded to be paid five months of unpaid wages. The director of the utility company, Ali Aliev, confirmed to Radio

Ozodi that the employees had not been paid, noting that he also did not get his salary and that the salaries comes from the regional budget. On January 12, the General Prosecutor of Kulob district told Radio Liberty that the local government issued a partial payment to the utility company in order to pay a portion of the employee salaries.

Collective bargaining contracts covered 90 percent of workers in the formal sector. In some cases foreign, specifically Chinese, workers received preferable treatment to local workers in labor disputes.

The government fully controlled trade unions and other labor unions. There were no reports of threats or violence by government entities toward trade unions; however, fearing government retaliation, unions made only limited demands regarding workers' rights. Most workers' grievances were resolved with union mediation between employee and employer.

Labor NGOs not designated as labor organizations played a minimal role in worker rights, as they were restricted from operating fully and freely.

b. Prohibition of Forced or Compulsory Labor

The law prohibits all forms of forced or compulsory labor, including that of children, except in cases defined in law. Resources, inspections, and remediation were inadequate. The law prohibits both forced sexual exploitation and forced labor; it prescribes penalties of five to 15 years' imprisonment. These penalties were sufficiently stringent and commensurate with other serious crimes, such as rape, and sufficient to deter violations.

The government continued to make progress in reducing the use of forced labor in the annual cotton harvest, although it still occurred. The Ministry of Labor, together with NGO representatives, conducted a monitoring mission of the cotton harvest during the year.

On January 5, the Interior Ministry's website reported that police arrested two women--one from Rudaki District and another 37-year-old woman from Vakhsh district--in Dushanbe who were allegedly involved in trafficking young women to the United Arab Emirates. In November 2014, they took a 23-year-old woman from the Khuroson district to Dubai where they forced her into prostitution. The reports noted that the arrested women collected USD 65,000 by prostituting the

TIP victim. A criminal proceeding was initiated against the two women. The ministry has not reported about the progress of the investigation.

In April, a 19-year-old resident of Rogun District, Qiyomiddin Sharifov, died after jumping into the Vakhsh River while running from military recruitment authorities trying to force him into military service. On May 19, the State Committee on Emergency Situations reported to the media that they were unable to locate Sharifov's body and had to suspend the rescue operation because of poor weather conditions.

See also the Department of State's *Trafficking in Persons Report* at www.state.gov/j/tip/rls/tiprpt/.

c. Prohibition of Child Labor and Minimum Age for Employment

The minimum age for children to work is 16 years, although children may work at age 15 with permission from the local trade union. By law children younger than age 18 may work no more than six hours a day and 36 hours per week. Children as young as age seven may participate in household labor and agricultural work, which is separately classified as family assistance. Many children younger than age 10 worked in bazaars or sold goods on the street. The highest incidences of child labor were in the domestic and agricultural sectors.

Enforcement of child labor laws is the responsibility of the Prosecutor General's Office, Ministry of Justice, Ministry of Social Welfare, Ministry of Internal Affairs, and appropriate local and regional governmental offices. Unions also are responsible for reporting any violations in the employment of minors. Citizens can bring unresolved cases involving child labor between unions and employers before the prosecutor general for investigation. There were few reports of violations because most children worked under the family assistance exception. There were reports that military recruitment authorities kidnapped children under the age of 18 from public places and subjected them to compulsory military service to fulfill local recruitment quotas.

The government enforced labor laws and worked with the International Organization for Migration to prevent the use of forced child labor in the autumn cotton harvest. Nevertheless, there were isolated reports that some children were exploited in agriculture. The overall instances of forced child labor in the cotton harvest decreased dramatically since 2013; the 2013 IOM annual assessment showed local or national government authorities responded to most cases. The government levied nine fines against employers using child labor and collected a total of 7,200 somoni ($900) from violators.

The Inter-ministerial Commission to Combat Trafficking in Persons disseminated a directive to local officials reiterating existing prohibitions and ordered the Labor Inspector's office to conduct a monitoring mission of the cotton-picking season. According to the IOM, however, no independent monitoring of the cotton harvest was conducted this year.

Also see the Department of Labor's *Findings on the Worst Forms of Child Labor* at www.dol.gov/ilab/reports/child-labor/findings.

d. Discrimination with Respect to Employment and Occupation

The law prohibits discrimination with respect to employment and occupation on the basis of race, sex, gender, disability, language, HIV-positive status, other communicable diseases, or social status. The law does not expressly prohibit worker discrimination on the basis of color, religion, political opinion, national origin or citizenship, or age. There were no official complaints of such discrimination with respect to employment and occupation. Nevertheless, employers discriminated against individuals based on sexual orientation and HIV-positive status, and police generally did not enforce these laws. LGBTI persons and HIV-positive individuals opted not to file complaints due to fear of harassment from law enforcement and the belief that police would not take action.

The law provides that women receive equal pay as men for equal work, but cultural barriers continued to restrict the professional opportunities available to women. Employers forced women to work overtime without additional pay.

e. Acceptable Conditions of Work

In June the president signed a decree to increase wages, pensions, and stipends starting July 1. According to new estimates, the minimum monthly wage in August was 400 somoni ($50), and the minimum monthly pension was 156 somoni ($20).

As of January 2015, the government defined the minimum standard of living as a basket of goods equal to 435 somoni ($55) per month. The government did not declare a formal poverty line.

The State Inspectorate for Supervision of Labor, Migration, and Employment under the Ministry of Labor is the responsible body for the overall supervision of enforcing labor law in the country. The Ministry of Finance enforces financial aspects of the labor law, and the Agency of Financial Control of the presidential administration oversees other aspects of the law. There is no legal prohibition on excessive compulsory overtime. The law mandates overtime payment, with the first two hours paid at a time-and-a-half rate and the remainder at double the rate. Resources, inspections, and remediation to enforce the law were inadequate. The State Inspectorate conducts inspections once every two years. Penalties for violations, including fines of 800 to 1,200 somoni ($100 to $150) were adequate, but the regulation was not enforced, and the government did not pay its employees for overtime work. Overtime payment was inconsistent in all sectors of the labor force.

The State Inspectorate for Supervision of Labor, Migration, and Employment is also responsible for enforcing health and safety standards. The government did not fully comply with these standards, partly because of corruption and the low salaries paid to inspectors. The law provides workers the right to remove themselves from hazardous working conditions without fear of loss of employment, but workers seldom exercised this right.

Farmers and agricultural workers, accounting for more than 60 percent of employment in the country, continued to work under difficult circumstances. There was no system to monitor or regulate working conditions in the agricultural and informal sector. Wages in agricultural sector are lowest among all other sectors, and many workers received payment in kind. The government's failure to ensure and protect land tenure rights continued to limit its ability to protect agricultural workers' rights.